ITALY TRAVEL GUIDE

2024-2025

Discover the Hidden Gems, Iconic Attractions, and Local Experiences

SERGIUS ALBERT

Copyright © 2024 by Austin kelly

All Rights Reserved

No part of this book may be reproduced, distributed, or transmitted in any form or by any means, including photocopying, recording, or other electronic or mechanical methods, without the prior written permission of the publisher, except in the case of brief quotations embodied in critical reviews and certain other noncommercial uses permitted by copyright law.

TABLE OF CONTENTS

INTRODUCTION   7
   Welcome to Italy   7
   How to Use This Guide   10

CHAPTER 1: GETTING TO ITALY   19
   Air Travel   20
   Train Travel   27
   Driving to Italy   31

CHAPTER 2: ACCOMMODATIONS   41
   Luxury Hotels   42
   Budget Stays   46
   Unique Lodgings   50

CHAPTER 3: CULINARY DELIGHTS   56
   Iconic Foods and Where to Find Them   57
   Italy's Best Restaurants   63
   Food Markets and Street Food   67

CHAPTER 4: MUST-SEE ATTRACTIONS 71
    Historical Landmarks   72

    Museums and Galleries   76

    Family-Friendly Activities   81

CHAPTER 5: CULTURE AND HISTORY 85

    Italy's Rich History   86

    Cultural Festivals and Events   93

    Local Arts and Music   97

CHAPTER 6: ADVENTURE AND RECREATION   101

    Parks and Outdoor Activities   102

    Water Sports and Boat Tours   106

    Day Trips from Italy   110

CHAPTER 7: SHOPPING IN ITALY 115

    Popular Shopping Districts   116

    Local Crafts and Souvenirs   120

    Shopping Tips and Tricks   123

CHAPTER 8: NIGHTLIFE AND ENTERTAINMENT   129

    Best Bars and Clubs   130

    Live Music and Performances   135

Night Tours and Experiences 138

CHAPTER 9: TRANSPORTATION WITHIN ITALY 142

Public Transit System 143

Bike and Scooter Rentals 152

Tips for Navigating Cities 157

CHAPTER 10: PRACTICAL INFORMATION 167

Currency, Banking, and ATMs 168

Health and Safety Tips 173

Useful Apps and Resources 178

CHAPTER 11: LOCAL CUSTOMS AND ETIQUETTE 185

1. Do's and Don'ts 186

2. Tipping and Manners 191

Language Basics 195

CHAPTER 12: SEASONAL CONSIDERATIONS 200

Best Times to Visit 201

What to Pack 207

Weather Conditions 211

CHAPTER 13. CONCLUSION 216

Credit@googlemaps

INTRODUCTION

Credit@google

Welcome to Italy

Italy, a land steeped in ancient history, artistic masterpieces, and breathtaking landscapes, beckons travelers from all corners of the globe. From the bustling streets of Rome to the serene countryside of Tuscany, Italy offers an unparalleled blend of cultural experiences, iconic landmarks, and world-renowned cuisine. Whether you're a first-time visitor or a seasoned traveler, Italy will captivate you with its blend of old-world charm and modern vitality.

Italy is more than just a destination; it's a mosaic of diverse regions, each offering its own unique charm and history. In the north, you'll find the chic urban centers of Milan and Turin, while the scenic Alps form a majestic backdrop. The central regions boast cultural and historical treasures like Florence, the birthplace of the Renaissance, and Rome, the eternal city whose ruins tell the story of the Roman

Empire. In the south, you'll discover coastal beauty along the Amalfi Coast, the volcanic wonders of Sicily, and the ancient trulli houses in Puglia.

In this travel guide, we'll take you on a journey through Italy's most iconic cities, hidden villages, and natural wonders. Whether you want to immerse yourself in the rich history of the Colosseum, relax on the beaches of Sardinia, hike the dramatic Dolomites, or indulge in the culinary delights of Naples, this guide is designed to provide you with all the information you need to make the most of your visit.

From art lovers to outdoor adventurers, foodies to history buffs, Italy offers something for everyone. In preparing for your journey, we hope this guide will inspire you to explore Italy's endless wonders with curiosity, respect, and a sense of adventure.

How to Use This Guide

The Italy Travel Guide 2024-2025 is your comprehensive companion for exploring the diverse landscapes, cultures, and attractions of Italy. This guide has been thoughtfully organized to ensure that you have easy access to the information you need, whether you're planning your itinerary in advance or navigating the country on the go.

Here's how to make the most of this guide:

1. **Planning Your Trip**

Use the guide to structure your travel plans from the start. Each chapter is organized to provide a step-by-step breakdown of the key aspects of your visit. Whether you're looking for accommodation, transportation options, or insider tips on where to eat, each section covers vital information to help you make informed decisions. The guide also includes details on when and where to go, based on seasonal conditions and festivals, so you can align your trip with Italy's best experiences.

2. **Detailed City and Regional Profiles**

Italy is made up of 20 distinct regions, each with its own culture, dialect, and attractions. This guide divides Italy into key regions and cities to help you focus on the areas that appeal most to your interests. Each chapter delves into Italy's major cities such as Rome, Venice, and Florence, but also introduces lesser-known destinations like the hilltop towns of Umbria, the vineyards of Piedmont, and the islands of Sicily and Sardinia.

For each region or city, we provide a comprehensive breakdown of the following:

- Must-see landmarks: From UNESCO World Heritage sites to local hidden gems.

- Accommodation options: Including luxury hotels, boutique stays, and budget-friendly choices.

- Culinary recommendations: Discover the best restaurants, local food markets, and street vendors for an authentic Italian dining experience.

- Activities and experiences: Whether you're interested in art galleries, outdoor adventures, or local festivals, the guide covers various attractions and activities for all types of travelers.

3. **Practical Travel Tips**

Traveling in Italy can present unique challenges, from navigating public transportation to understanding local customs. To ensure a smooth and enjoyable trip, the guide provides practical advice, such as:

- Transportation: Information on getting around Italy, from high-speed trains and car rentals to local buses and bike rentals. We also provide advice on how to navigate Italy's sometimes chaotic road systems and city centers.

- Language and communication: While many Italians in tourist areas speak English, learning a few essential Italian phrases can enhance your experience. Our guide offers basic Italian vocabulary and phrases to help you communicate effectively.

- Currency and tipping: Italy uses the Euro (€), and tipping is not as prevalent as in some other countries. We explain local practices for tipping in restaurants, taxis, and hotels, as well as how to handle currency exchanges and payments.

- Health and safety: Tips on how to stay safe, what to do in case of an emergency, and advice on health precautions, including access to pharmacies, healthcare services, and travel insurance recommendations.

4. **Cultural Insights**

Italy's cultural heritage is vast, from its art and architecture to its social customs. Throughout this guide, you'll find insights into Italy's cultural traditions, whether it's understanding the significance of Italian festivals or observing local etiquette, such as how to dress when visiting churches or dining in local restaurants. These cultural insights will help you engage more deeply with the local people and traditions, ensuring you experience the true essence of Italy.

5. Seasonal Considerations

Italy is a country for all seasons, with each time of year offering a unique set of experiences. The guide provides detailed information about what to expect in terms of weather, crowd levels, and seasonal activities. Whether you're planning a summer holiday along the Amalfi Coast or a winter escape to the Alps, the guide will help you pack accordingly and plan your activities to suit the season.

6. Sustainability and Responsible Travel

As tourism continues to grow in Italy, being mindful of your environmental and cultural impact is increasingly important. This guide includes recommendations on how to travel sustainably, from supporting local businesses and artisans to minimizing your environmental footprint. We also encourage responsible tourism, such as respecting historical sites, contributing to the preservation of natural landscapes, and being conscious of overtourism in popular areas.

7. **Digital Resources and Tools**

Throughout the guide, you'll find references to helpful apps and websites that can assist you with booking accommodation, checking transportation schedules, and finding local recommendations.

Whether it's accessing Italy's public transportation apps, finding walking tours, or using translation tools, we've compiled a list of digital resources that will make your trip smoother and more enjoyable.

By using this guide, you'll have a valuable resource at your fingertips that will help you navigate Italy's diverse landscapes, cities, and cultural landmarks. Whether you're looking for practical advice or inspiration for your next adventure, the Italy Travel Guide 2024-2025 is here to ensure you have an unforgettable experience.

CHAPTER 1: GETTING TO ITALY

Credit@google

Italy, located in southern Europe, is a destination that is easily accessible from all over the world. Depending on where you're coming from, your preferred mode of travel, and the experiences you want to have along the way, there are several ways to get to Italy. This chapter provides a comprehensive overview of the different transportation options available to help you reach Italy—whether by air, train, or car and gives practical tips on navigating each mode of travel.

Air Travel

For most international travelers, flying is the fastest and most convenient way to reach Italy. Italy is well connected with major airports in several cities that serve as gateways to the country, making it easy to arrive no matter where you're coming from.

Major International Airports

Italy has several international airports spread across its regions. These are the main hubs for international flights, providing convenient access to different parts of the country:

- Leonardo da Vinci–Fiumicino Airport (FCO), Rome: Italy's largest and busiest airport, Fiumicino, is located about 32 kilometers southwest of central Rome. It handles flights from major international cities around the world. As Rome is centrally located, this airport is a great entry point for travelers planning to explore various parts of the country.

- Milan Malpensa Airport (MXP), Milan: Serving northern Italy, Malpensa is Milan's primary international airport and is particularly convenient for travelers heading to Lombardy, the Italian Lakes, or the Alps. It's also a major hub for business travelers.

- Venice Marco Polo Airport (VCE), Venice: Located near Venice, this airport is perfect for visitors planning to explore the iconic canals, nearby regions like Veneto, or cities like Verona.

- Naples International Airport (NAP), Naples: A great starting point for exploring southern Italy, including the Amalfi Coast, Pompeii, and the islands of Capri and Ischia.

- Florence Airport (FLR), Florence: Though smaller, Florence's airport is convenient for those wanting to head straight into Tuscany and explore the Renaissance city of Florence and the surrounding countryside.

- Bologna Guglielmo Marconi Airport (BLQ), Bologna: Ideal for travelers interested in visiting the Emilia-Romagna region, known for its culinary heritage and historic cities like Bologna, Modena, and Parma.

- Catania–Fontanarossa Airport (CTA), Sicily: Located on the east coast of Sicily, this airport is a gateway to the island's volcanic landscapes, ancient ruins, and vibrant culture.

- Olbia Costa Smeralda Airport (OLB), Sardinia: For those headed to the beautiful island of Sardinia, Olbia is the most convenient entry point, particularly for exploring the Costa Smeralda.

Booking Flights

Italy is well connected by numerous international airlines, including major carriers like Alitalia (Italy's national airline), Lufthansa, British Airways, Air France, and many low-cost airlines like Ryanair and

EasyJet. It's advisable to book your flights well in advance, especially if you plan to travel during the peak tourist season, which runs from late spring to early autumn. Flight comparison websites and apps like Skyscanner, Google Flights, and Momondo are helpful tools for finding the best deals.

Arrival and Immigration

Upon arriving in Italy, if you're coming from outside the European Union (EU), you'll need to go through passport control. Make sure your passport is valid for at least six months beyond your planned date of departure from Italy. For most travelers from the US, Canada, Australia, and many other countries, a visa is not required for stays of up to 90 days, as Italy is part of the Schengen

Agreement. However, it's essential to check the latest visa requirements based on your nationality.

Once you clear customs, airports in Italy are well-equipped with transportation options, including taxis, airport shuttles, buses, and trains, to help you reach your final destination.

Domestic Flights

If you're flying into one of Italy's major international airports but plan to visit another part of the country, you may want to consider taking a domestic flight. Several airlines operate domestic routes within Italy, including Alitalia, Volotea, and Ryanair. This option can save time, especially if you're traveling from northern to southern Italy, or vice versa.

Train Travel

Italy is part of Europe's extensive rail network, and traveling to Italy by train is an excellent option, especially if you're already in Europe. The Italian train system is renowned for its efficiency, comfort, and coverage. High-speed trains connect Italy to neighboring countries like France, Switzerland, Austria, and Germany, making train travel a scenic and convenient way to arrive.

High-Speed International Trains

Several high-speed train services connect Italy to major cities in Europe. These trains offer a comfortable and scenic alternative to air travel, with the added benefit of arriving directly in the heart of Italy's major cities.

- Thello Trains: Operating between France and Italy, Thello offers services from Paris to Milan, and from Nice to major Italian cities such as Milan, Venice, and Rome. The trains are comfortable and allow for overnight journeys if you want to travel while you sleep.

- TGV InOui (France): The TGV high-speed trains link Paris and Lyon to Turin and Milan, with direct services taking just over 7 hours from Paris to Milan. It's a great option if you prefer not to fly and want to enjoy the views of the French and Italian countryside.

- EuroCity (Switzerland): EuroCity trains connect Swiss cities like Zurich, Geneva, and Basel with Italian destinations including Milan, Venice, and Florence. The scenic routes pass through the Swiss Alps, offering stunning vistas along the way.

- ÖBB Nightjet (Austria and Germany): This night train service connects Vienna, Munich, and other major European cities with Italian destinations such as Venice, Rome, and Milan. Traveling overnight can be a comfortable and time-saving option, especially on longer routes.

Booking Train Tickets

Booking train tickets is straightforward and can be done through several online platforms, including Trenitalia (Italy's national railway), Italo (a private high-speed train company), and international booking platforms like Trainline or Eurail. Booking in advance often ensures better prices and guarantees seating, especially during busy travel seasons. It's also worth exploring rail passes such as the Eurail Pass, which can offer flexibility if you're planning to travel to multiple countries within Europe.

Border Crossings

Traveling to Italy by train from another Schengen Area country means you won't have to go through passport control at the border. However, trains from non-Schengen countries, such as the UK, may require passport checks. It's always wise to keep your travel documents accessible during the journey.

Driving to Italy

For travelers who enjoy road trips and the freedom to explore at their own pace, driving to Italy is a fantastic option. Italy's extensive road network connects to neighboring countries through major highways and scenic routes, offering flexibility and the opportunity to discover hidden gems along the way.

Routes into Italy

Italy shares land borders with several countries, including France, Switzerland, Austria, and Slovenia. The major highways and tunnels linking Italy to these countries make for easy and picturesque road trips.

France to Italy: The drive from France to Italy is particularly popular among travelers exploring both countries. The Mont Blanc Tunnel connects Chamonix in France to the Aosta Valley in northern Italy. Alternatively, the French Riviera offers coastal routes leading into Liguria, where you can drive to cities like Genoa or the Cinque Terre.

- Switzerland to Italy: The Gotthard Pass and the Gotthard Base Tunnel link Switzerland to Italy's northern region, with access to Milan and the Italian Lakes. The scenic Bernina Pass is another option for those heading to the Lombardy or Veneto regions.

- Austria to Italy: The Brenner Pass is the main route between Austria and Italy, connecting Innsbruck to the South Tyrol region. The drive takes you through alpine landscapes and offers easy access to cities like Bolzano and Trento.

- Slovenia to Italy: For those coming from Eastern Europe, the E61 highway links Slovenia to Italy, making Trieste a convenient entry point. This route is ideal for travelers heading to northeastern Italy, including Venice and Friuli Venezia Giulia.

Car Rentals and Documentation

If you're renting a car to drive into Italy, make sure you have all the necessary documentation:

- A valid driver's license (an International Driving Permit may be required depending on your country of origin).
- Proof of insurance, which is often included in your car rental agreement.
- A credit card for deposits and toll payments.

Italy's road system is well maintained, and the major highways (known as autostrade) are modern and efficient. However, they are also toll roads, so be prepared to pay tolls using cash or a credit card.

What to Expect When Driving in Italy

- Traffic and Parking: Italy's roads can be busy, especially around major cities and during peak tourist seasons. Parking in cities can be challenging, so many travelers opt to park on the outskirts and take public transportation into city centers.

- ZTL (Limited Traffic Zones): Many historic cities in Italy, such as Rome, Florence, and Venice, have Zona a Traffico Limitato (ZTL), where only residents and authorized vehicles can enter during specific hours. Be aware of these zones to avoid hefty fines.

- Scenic Drives: Driving into Italy provides access to some of the most scenic routes in Europe. Whether you're navigating the coastal roads of the Amalfi Coast, meandering through the rolling hills of Tuscany, or driving through the Dolomites in northern Italy, the opportunity to explore Italy's landscapes at your own pace is a unique experience. Below are some iconic road trip routes:

- Amalfi Coast: The narrow, winding road along the coast between Positano and Amalfi offers dramatic views of the Mediterranean and is considered one of the most scenic drives in the world. However, it can be busy and challenging due to the tight turns and heavy traffic, particularly in summer.

Tuscany: Driving through Tuscany's countryside is a dream, with its rolling hills, vineyards, olive groves, and medieval hill towns like Siena and San Gimignano. The Via Chiantigiana (SR222) is a beautiful route that takes you through the heart of the Chianti wine region.

- Italian Alps: The roads through the Dolomites are both scenic and exhilarating. The Great Dolomites Road connects Bolzano to Cortina d'Ampezzo and offers stunning views of mountain peaks, valleys, and alpine meadows.

Border Crossings and Regulations

Driving into Italy from other European countries is generally hassle-free, as Italy is part of the Schengen Agreement, meaning there are no formal border checks between Italy and other Schengen member states. However, it's important to carry your passport or ID, driver's license, car rental documents, and insurance at all times in case of random checks or emergencies.

If you're coming from a non-EU country, you should familiarize yourself with the driving laws and regulations in Italy. Keep in mind that driving is on the right-hand side, and seat belts are mandatory for all passengers. It's also a legal requirement to carry a warning triangle, a reflective vest, and spare light bulbs in your vehicle.

Fuel Stations and Roadside Assistance

Italy has numerous fuel stations along major highways and rural roads, and most operate 24/7, especially on the autostrade. Some stations, particularly in smaller towns or villages, may close for a few hours in the afternoon, so plan your fuel stops accordingly. Roadside assistance is readily available, and most rental car companies provide emergency services in case of breakdowns or accidents.

Whether you're flying, taking the train, or driving, getting to Italy is a seamless experience thanks to its modern infrastructure and connections with other countries. Each mode of travel offers its own unique perspective, from the quick convenience of air travel to the scenic landscapes you'll pass by train or car. No matter how you choose to arrive, your journey to Italy is just the beginning of an unforgettable adventure through this culturally rich and geographically diverse country.

CHAPTER 2: ACCOMMODATIONS

Credit@google

Italy offers a vast range of accommodations that cater to every type of traveler, from luxury seekers to budget-conscious adventurers. Whether you're dreaming of a stay in a lavish palace, a charming bed-and-breakfast, or a unique historical dwelling, Italy's diverse lodging options promise an unforgettable experience. In this chapter, we'll explore the various types of accommodations available, providing insights into what you can expect from each, no matter your budget or style.

Luxury Hotels

Italy is synonymous with style, sophistication, and timeless elegance, and this extends to its luxury hotels. From historic palazzos in the heart of bustling cities to five-star coastal resorts, Italy's luxury hotels provide a perfect blend of classic charm and modern amenities. These hotels offer not just a place to stay but an indulgent experience where every detail is carefully curated.

What to Expect from Luxury Hotels

- World-Class Service: Expect exceptional service, from personal concierges who can arrange exclusive tours and reservations, to highly attentive staff anticipating your every need.

- Prime Locations: Most luxury hotels are centrally located near major landmarks, cultural sites, or scenic spots, offering guests easy access to the highlights of each city or region.

- Amenities: Top-notch facilities are a hallmark of Italy's luxury accommodations. You can expect high-end restaurants, often featuring Michelin-starred chefs, spa and wellness centers, private pools, and even curated experiences like wine tastings or art tours.

- Notable Luxury Hotels:
  - Rome: The Hotel Hassler near the Spanish Steps offers grand suites with stunning city views, while the St. Regis Rome merges historical elegance with modern luxury.

  - Florence: The Four Seasons Hotel Firenze is located in a restored Renaissance palazzo, set amidst beautiful gardens, offering a sanctuary within the city.

- Venice: The Belmond Hotel Cipriani, located on Giudecca Island, offers lavish accommodations with breathtaking views of the Venetian lagoon.

Luxury on the Coast

For those seeking a more coastal experience, the Amalfi Coast and Lake Como regions provide some of Italy's most exclusive properties. On the Amalfi Coast, Le Sirenuse in Positano offers Mediterranean charm with world-class service, while Villa d'Este on Lake Como offers a grand estate with centuries of history and magnificent lake views.

Budget Stays

Traveling on a budget in Italy doesn't mean compromising on comfort or charm. Budget-friendly accommodations are available throughout the country, ranging from quaint bed-and-breakfasts to affordable guesthouses and well-maintained hostels. These options allow travelers to experience Italy's beauty and culture without breaking the bank.

What to Expect from Budget Stays

- Affordable Comfort: Budget hotels, hostels, and guesthouses in Italy often provide clean, comfortable rooms, and essential amenities like free Wi-Fi, air conditioning, and complimentary breakfasts.

- Family-Run Properties: Many budget accommodations, especially in smaller towns and rural areas, are family-run. These lodgings often offer a personal touch, where guests are treated like family, and hosts are eager to share local knowledge and tips.

- Convenient Locations: While budget accommodations in large cities may not be directly in the city center, many are located in nearby neighborhoods with easy access to public transportation.

- Popular Budget Options:

  - Rome: The Beehive Hostel is a popular choice for budget-conscious travelers offering private rooms and dormitories with a relaxed, welcoming atmosphere.

  - Florence: Hotel Dali provides affordable, centrally located accommodation, perfect for those wanting to explore the city's museums and galleries on foot.

- Venice: Hotel ai Tolentini, a short walk from Venice's Piazzale Roma, offers simple yet comfortable rooms at an affordable rate.

Hostels and B&Bs

For those who enjoy social atmospheres and meeting other travelers, hostels are a great option. Italian hostels often feature shared dormitories and private rooms, providing an affordable way to explore major cities. Bed-and-breakfasts (B&Bs) are also popular, especially in the countryside, offering homey lodgings with a personal touch, often including a delicious homemade breakfast.

Unique Lodgings

One of the joys of traveling in Italy is the opportunity to stay in unique accommodations that offer more than just a place to sleep—they provide a chance to truly experience Italy's history, culture, and natural beauty. From medieval castles to rural farmhouses, Italy's unique lodging options make for a memorable stay.

Agriturismo (Farm Stays)

Agriturismo, or farm stays, are an increasingly popular choice, especially for those exploring Italy's countryside. These lodgings are often located on working farms or vineyards, giving guests a glimpse into rural Italian life. Many agriturismi offer farm-to-table dining, with meals made from ingredients grown on-site, as well as activities like cooking classes, wine tasting, and guided tours of the property.

- Notable Agriturismi:

  - Agriturismo Poggio ai Santi in Tuscany offers guests stunning views of the countryside, luxurious rooms, and home-cooked meals made from organic produce grown on the farm.

  - Masseria Il Frantoio in Puglia combines rustic charm with elegant accommodations, offering olive oil tastings and traditional Apulian cuisine.

Castles and Historical Properties

For travelers seeking a more historical stay, Italy offers numerous opportunities to sleep in ancient castles, restored palazzos, and monasteries. These properties combine old-world charm with modern amenities, allowing guests to immerse themselves in Italy's history while enjoying contemporary comforts.

- Stay in a Castle:

  - Castello di Petroia, near Gubbio in Umbria, is a 12th-century castle where you can experience medieval architecture while enjoying luxurious suites and gourmet dining.

- Castello di Pavone in Piedmont provides guests with an authentic castle experience, complete with towers, drawbridges, and period furnishings.

Trulli and Cave Hotels

In Puglia, travelers can experience a unique stay in trulli, traditional stone huts with conical roofs. These distinctive structures offer a rustic yet comfortable stay in the heart of the Puglian countryside. In Matera, visitors can stay in cave hotels, built into the ancient Sassi cave dwellings, offering a rare and immersive experience in this UNESCO World Heritage site.

- Unique Stays:

- Trulli Holiday Resort in Alberobello offers guests the chance to stay in beautifully restored trulli, blending ancient architecture with modern amenities.

- Sextantio Le Grotte della Civita in Matera is a luxurious cave hotel that allows guests to experience the unique atmosphere of the ancient city while enjoying upscale accommodations.

Italy's diverse range of accommodations ensures that every traveler can find a place to stay that meets their needs, whether they seek the opulence of a five-star hotel, the charm of a countryside B&B, or the uniqueness of a centuries-old castle. The country's rich history, natural beauty, and emphasis on hospitality are reflected in its lodging options, providing not just a place to rest but an essential part of the Italian experience. No matter where you choose to stay, Italy's accommodations promise to enhance your journey through this captivating country.

CHAPTER 3: CULINARY DELIGHTS

Credit@google

Italy is a land where food transcends sustenance and becomes an art form, a deep cultural expression, and an essential part of everyday life. Italian cuisine is globally renowned, and each region boasts its own specialties and iconic dishes. From simple street food to world-class fine dining, Italy offers a gastronomic journey that is as varied as it is delicious. In this chapter, we will explore Italy's iconic foods, the best restaurants, and the bustling food markets and street food that reflect the heart and soul of Italian culinary tradition.

Iconic Foods and Where to Find Them

Italy is famed for its regional dishes, many of which have become culinary symbols of the country worldwide. Yet, to truly experience Italian cuisine, you must explore the unique flavors of each region, savoring the local specialties in the places where they were born. Here's a guide to some of Italy's most iconic dishes and the best regions to try them.

Pasta and Risotto

- Spaghetti alla Carbonara (Rome): One of Italy's most famous pasta dishes, spaghetti alla carbonara is a rich combination of eggs, pecorino cheese, guanciale (cured pork cheek), and black pepper. Rome is the birthplace of this dish, and some of the best places to try it include Trattoria Da Enzo al 29 and Roscioli.

- Tagliatelle al Ragù (Bologna): Often misnamed as "spaghetti Bolognese" outside Italy, the authentic version of this dish is served with tagliatelle, not spaghetti, and features a hearty, slow-cooked meat sauce. The city of Bologna, in the Emilia-Romagna region, is the best place to enjoy it. Visit Osteria dell'Orsa or Trattoria Anna Maria for an authentic experience.

- Risotto alla Milanese (Milan): This creamy risotto, flavored with saffron, is one of Milan's signature dishes. It is often served with ossobuco, a slow-cooked veal shank. Head to Ristorante Il Marchesino or Trattoria del Nuovo Macello to sample this luxurious dish in Milan.

Pizza and Focaccia

- Pizza Napoletana (Naples): Naples is the birthplace of the iconic Neapolitan pizza, characterized by its thin, soft, and slightly chewy crust with simple yet flavorful toppings. The classic Margherita (tomato, mozzarella, and basil) is a must-try. Famous pizzerias in Naples include L'Antica Pizzeria da Michele and Pizzeria Sorbillo, both of which have achieved near-legendary status.

- Focaccia (Liguria): Liguria is the home of focaccia, a deliciously soft and airy flatbread, often topped with olive oil, salt, or herbs. In the coastal town of Genoa, you can enjoy fresh focaccia in countless bakeries, with Focacceria da Marinetta being a top recommendation.

Meats and Seafood

- Bistecca alla Fiorentina (Florence): This massive T-bone steak, cooked rare and served on the bone, is a Tuscan specialty. The steak is typically sourced from the prized Chianina breed of cattle. For a classic Tuscan steak experience, visit Trattoria Mario or Osteria di Giovanni in Florence.

- Frutti di Mare (Amalfi Coast): Italy's coastal regions are renowned for their fresh seafood, and the Amalfi Coast is a paradise for lovers of frutti di mare (seafood dishes). Whether it's clams, mussels, or squid, the seafood here is some of the freshest in the country. Restaurants like Il Pirata in Praiano or Ristorante Marina Grande in Amalfi offer incredible seafood platters with a stunning view of the Mediterranean.

Cheese and Cured Meats

- Parmigiano-Reggiano (Emilia-Romagna): Known as the "King of Cheeses," Parmigiano-Reggiano is a staple of Italian cuisine. The best way to experience this cheese is to visit a local dairy in the Emilia-Romagna region, particularly in Parma. Here, you can sample freshly aged Parmigiano-Reggiano straight from the source.

- Prosciutto di Parma (Parma): This delicately cured ham, produced in the Parma region, is another famous Italian delicacy. A visit to Parma offers an opportunity to tour the prosciuttifici (ham factories), where you can learn about the aging process and sample the delicious ham.

Italy's Best Restaurants

Italy's culinary scene is vast and varied, offering dining experiences that range from casual trattorias to Michelin-starred restaurants. No matter where you travel in Italy, you'll find restaurants that celebrate the country's rich culinary heritage while also pushing the boundaries of innovation.

Michelin-Starred Restaurants

Italy is home to many Michelin-starred restaurants, where top chefs create culinary masterpieces inspired by both tradition and innovation. Some of the country's most renowned dining establishments include:

- Osteria Francescana (Modena): Helmed by celebrated chef Massimo Bottura, Osteria Francescana has been consistently ranked as one of the best restaurants in the world. Bottura's inventive approach to Italian cuisine reimagines traditional flavors in modern, creative ways. Reservations are essential, and dining here is an unforgettable experience.

- Enoteca Pinchiorri (Florence): This three-star Michelin restaurant offers exquisite Tuscan cuisine with a contemporary twist. Located in the heart of Florence, Enoteca Pinchiorri is known for its exceptional wine cellar, which houses one of the largest collections of fine wines in Europe.

- La Pergola (Rome): La Pergola is Rome's only three-star Michelin restaurant, offering breathtaking views of the city from its location atop Monte Mario. Chef Heinz Beck creates innovative Mediterranean dishes using the finest local ingredients, making it one of the top dining destinations in Italy.

Traditional Trattorias and Osterias

While Michelin-starred restaurants offer high-end dining experiences, Italy's trattorias and osterias are where you'll find authentic, heartwarming Italian cuisine at its best. These restaurants often serve regional dishes made with local ingredients, providing a more casual but no less delicious experience.

- Da Cesare al Casaletto (Rome): Known for its classic Roman dishes like cacio e pepe and saltimbocca alla romana, Da Cesare al Casaletto is a beloved trattoria where locals go for a comforting meal.

- Trattoria Sostanza (Florence): This historic eatery in Florence is famous for its pollo al burro (butter chicken) and bistecca alla Fiorentina. Trattoria Sostanza has been serving traditional Tuscan fare for over a century, making it a must-visit for food lovers.

- Osteria Antica Marina (Catania): Located in Sicily, this osteria offers the freshest seafood dishes, sourced daily from the nearby fish market. The menu features Sicilian favorites like pasta alla norma and sarde a beccafico (stuffed sardines).

Food Markets and Street Food

One of the best ways to experience Italy's culinary culture is to visit its bustling food markets and street food vendors. These vibrant spaces are where locals shop for fresh ingredients and where visitors can sample a wide array of regional delicacies.

Famous Food Markets

- Mercato di San Lorenzo (Florence): Florence's central market is a food lover's paradise, offering fresh produce, meats, cheeses, and prepared foods. The market is a great place to sample Tuscan specialties like lampredotto (a tripe sandwich) or buy ingredients for a picnic in the nearby Piazza della Repubblica.

- Mercato di Campo de' Fiori (Rome): One of Rome's oldest markets, Campo de' Fiori is located in the heart of the city and is known for its fresh vegetables, fruits, and aromatic herbs. This lively market is perfect for grabbing fresh ingredients or enjoying a slice of Roman pizza bianca on the go.

- La Vucciria (Palermo): In the heart of Palermo, La Vucciria market offers an authentic taste of Sicilian street food. From arancini (fried rice balls) to pane con la milza (spleen sandwich), this market is a haven for adventurous eaters.

Must-Try Street Food
- Supplì (Rome): These fried rice balls, similar to arancini, are filled with mozzarella and sometimes

ragù. Found in many Roman eateries, they are the perfect snack for a quick bite.

- Gelato (Nationwide): No visit to Italy is complete without indulging in gelato. Each region offers its own variations, but some of the best gelaterias include Gelateria dei Neri in Florence, Gelateria La Carraia in Rome, and Venchi in Milan.

- Farinata (Liguria): A savory chickpea pancake, farinata is a traditional Ligurian street food that's crispy on the outside and soft on the inside. Try it at a local bakery in Genoa or along the Ligurian coast.

CHAPTER 4: MUST-SEE ATTRACTIONS

Credit@google

Italy is a country steeped in history, art, and culture, offering an incredible array of attractions that span centuries. From ancient ruins to Renaissance masterpieces, its landmarks are some of the most iconic in the world. Whether you're a history buff, an art enthusiast, or a family looking for exciting activities, Italy has something to offer everyone. In this chapter, we'll explore Italy's historical landmarks, its world-class museums and galleries, and the many family-friendly activities that make Italy a must-visit destination.

Historical Landmarks

Italy is home to a rich and diverse array of historical sites, each telling a unique story of the country's past. From the ancient ruins of the Roman Empire to medieval castles and Renaissance palaces, Italy's historical landmarks are an essential part of any visit.

The Colosseum (Rome)

One of the most famous landmarks in the world, the Colosseum is a symbol of the might of the Roman Empire. Completed in 80 AD, this ancient amphitheater could hold up to 50,000 spectators and was used for gladiatorial contests and public spectacles. Today, the Colosseum is one of Italy's most visited attractions, offering guided tours that take you through its impressive architecture and history. Don't miss the Roman Forum, located nearby, which served as the center of public life in ancient Rome.

The Leaning Tower of Pisa (Pisa)

No trip to Italy is complete without seeing the Leaning Tower of Pisa. This iconic bell tower, famous for its unintended tilt, is part of the Piazza dei Miracoli, which also includes Pisa's cathedral and baptistery. Visitors can climb the 294 steps to the top of the tower for a unique perspective on the surrounding area.

Pompeii and Herculaneum (Naples)

These ancient cities were famously buried under volcanic ash when Mount Vesuvius erupted in 79 AD. Pompeii and Herculaneum offer an incredible window into life during the Roman Empire, with well-preserved ruins that include homes, temples, theaters, and bathhouses. A visit to these archaeological sites allows you to walk the streets as they were nearly 2,000 years ago, with many artifacts and frescoes still intact.

The Vatican and St. Peter's Basilica (Vatican City)

The Vatican is the spiritual and administrative center of the Roman Catholic Church and home to some of the world's most important religious and cultural sites. St. Peter's Basilica, the largest church in the world, is an architectural masterpiece that dominates the skyline of Vatican City. Visitors can explore its grand interior, including Michelangelo's Pietà, and climb to the top of the dome for breathtaking views of Rome.

The Duomo (Florence)

Florence's Cathedral of Santa Maria del Fiore, more commonly known as the Duomo, is a stunning example of Gothic architecture. Its magnificent dome, designed by Filippo Brunelleschi, was an engineering marvel of its time and remains one of the largest brick domes in the world. The cathedral's interior and its accompanying bell tower offer an unforgettable experience for visitors interested in Italy's Renaissance heritage.

Museums and Galleries

Italy's contribution to the world of art is immeasurable, and its museums and galleries are home to some of the most important works of art in history. From Renaissance paintings to modern installations, Italy's art scene is both historic and vibrant, with something for everyone.

The Uffizi Gallery (Florence)

As one of the most famous art museums in the world, the Uffizi Gallery houses an unrivaled collection of Renaissance masterpieces. The gallery's extensive collection includes works by Michelangelo, Leonardo da Vinci, Raphael, and Botticelli. One of its most famous pieces is Botticelli's The Birth of Venus, a stunning depiction of the goddess rising from the sea. A visit to the Uffizi is a must for any art lover.

The Vatican Museums (Vatican City)

The Vatican Museums contain an extraordinary collection of art and historical treasures gathered by the Catholic Church over centuries. The museums' highlights include the Sistine Chapel, with its famous ceiling painted by Michelangelo, as well as the Raphael Rooms and numerous classical sculptures. The breadth and diversity of the collection make this one of the most significant cultural institutions in the world.

Galleria Borghese (Rome)

Nestled in the heart of Rome, the Galleria Borghese is an intimate museum showcasing a collection of Baroque and Renaissance art. Highlights include works by Bernini, Caravaggio, Titian, and Canova. The museum is housed in a stunning villa surrounded by the Borghese Gardens, making it a perfect stop for both art and nature lovers.

Accademia Gallery (Florence)

The Accademia Gallery is home to Michelangelo's David, arguably the most famous sculpture in the world. This masterpiece of Renaissance art draws millions of visitors each year, who come to marvel at the perfection of its form and detail. In addition to David, the Accademia Gallery houses other works by Michelangelo and an impressive collection of Italian Renaissance art.

Museo Egizio (Turin)

For something a little different, the Museo Egizio in Turin offers a deep dive into the world of ancient Egypt. It is one of the largest collections of Egyptian artifacts outside of Egypt and includes mummies, statues, and ancient papyrus scrolls. This museum is perfect for families or those interested in ancient civilizations.

Family-Friendly Activities

Italy is a fantastic destination for families, offering a wide range of activities that cater to visitors of all ages. Whether you're exploring ancient ruins, enjoying nature, or indulging in gelato, Italy ensures that everyone in the family will have an unforgettable time.

Exploring Castles and Fortresses

Italy's landscape is dotted with ancient castles and fortresses that will captivate the imaginations of children and adults alike. From the towering Castel Sant'Angelo in Rome to the fairytale-like Castello di Sammezzano in Tuscany, there are plenty of opportunities for families to explore Italy's medieval past.

Venice's Gondola Rides

A trip to Venice wouldn't be complete without a scenic gondola ride through the city's famous canals. While Venice's historical attractions may appeal to adults, children will love the experience of gliding through the city's waterways, passing under its many bridges. The whole family can enjoy the beauty of Venice from the unique vantage point of a gondola.

Gardaland (Lake Garda)

For a day of fun and excitement, head to Gardaland, Italy's largest theme park located near

Lake Garda. With thrilling roller coasters, water rides, and live shows, Gardaland offers entertainment for the whole family. There's also an aquarium and a Peppa Pig Land area, making it ideal for younger children.

Italy's Beautiful Beaches

Italy is home to some of the most stunning beaches in Europe, and they're perfect for families looking to relax and enjoy the sun. The Amalfi Coast, Sardinia, and Sicily offer picturesque coastlines with crystal-clear waters and soft sand, ideal for swimming, snorkeling, and building sandcastles.

Exploring Natural Parks

For families who love the great outdoors, Italy's many national parks offer endless opportunities for hiking, wildlife spotting, and picnicking. Parks like Cinque Terre National Park and Gran Paradiso National Park provide stunning landscapes and accessible trails for visitors of all ages.

CHAPTER 5: CULTURE AND HISTORY

Credit@google

Italy is a country where history, art, and culture are woven into the very fabric of daily life. From the grandeur of the Roman Empire to the Renaissance, Italy has profoundly influenced the world in terms of culture, philosophy, and the arts. This chapter explores the richness of Italy's history, the vibrant cultural festivals and events that take place throughout the year, and the country's contributions to the world of local arts and music.

Italy's Rich History

Italy's history is one of the most remarkable in the world, with contributions to civilization that stretch back millennia. From the rise and fall of the Roman Empire to the birth of the Renaissance, Italy has been at the center of some of the world's most important historical and cultural moments. Understanding Italy's past is key to appreciating its art, architecture, and way of life today.

Ancient Italy and the Roman Empire

Italy's history can be traced back to the time of the Etruscans (circa 800-400 BC), a powerful civilization that thrived in the regions of modern-day Tuscany, Lazio, and Umbria. The Etruscans laid the foundation for many aspects of Roman culture, from engineering to religious practices.

However, the most significant chapter of ancient Italy's history begins with the rise of Rome. Founded in 753 BC, Rome grew from a small city-state to the heart of the vast Roman Empire. At its height, the empire spanned much of Europe, North Africa, and parts of Asia. Rome was the world's most powerful city, known for its innovations in law, architecture, governance, and warfare. Some of its most iconic structures—such as the Colosseum, Pantheon, and Roman Forum—still stand today as testament to its grandeur.

The Roman Empire's influence was unparalleled, and many of the legal, political, and architectural innovations of this era still shape the modern world. The fall of Rome in 476 AD marked the beginning of the Middle Ages, a time when Italy was fragmented into various city-states and kingdoms, often under the control of foreign powers such as the Byzantine Empire, the Holy Roman Empire, and the Normans.

The Middle Ages and the Rise of City-States

After the fall of the Roman Empire, Italy entered a period of political fragmentation and instability. However, this time also saw the rise of powerful city-states like Venice, Florence, Milan, and Genoa, which became important centers of trade, banking, and culture. These city-states often engaged in fierce rivalry, leading to wars and shifting alliances, but they also fostered an environment that allowed for the flourishing of the arts and sciences.

One of the most significant events during this time was the Crusades, in which many Italian city-states played a crucial role in providing ships and supplies for the Christian armies traveling to the Holy Land. The city of Venice, in particular, became one of the wealthiest and most powerful maritime republics in the world.

The Renaissance

Italy's most significant contribution to world history is undoubtedly the Renaissance, a period of unparalleled cultural rebirth that began in the 14th century and lasted until the 17th century. Florence is widely regarded as the birthplace of the Renaissance, thanks to the patronage of wealthy families like the Medici and the influence of artists, thinkers, and scientists such as Leonardo da Vinci, Michelangelo, Raphael, and Galileo.

During this period, Italy became the center of the world's artistic and intellectual life. Renaissance thinkers sought to revive the ideals of classical antiquity, emphasizing humanism, the potential of the individual, and the study of the natural world. The art and architecture of the Renaissance—characterized by perspective, proportion, and balance—still define much of Italy's cities today. Masterpieces such as the Sistine Chapel, David, and The Last Supper continue to attract millions of visitors.

Unification and Modern Italy

Italy remained a collection of independent states until the mid-19th century. The movement toward a unified Italy, known as the Risorgimento, was led by figures such as Giuseppe Garibaldi, Giuseppe Mazzini, and Count Cavour. The unification of Italy was officially completed in 1861, although Rome did not become the capital until 1870.

The 20th century saw Italy involved in both World Wars. After World War II, Italy became a republic, following the fall of Mussolini's Fascist regime. Since then, Italy has rebuilt itself into a vibrant, democratic country, now one of the most influential members of the European Union.

Cultural Festivals and Events

Italy's rich cultural calendar reflects the country's deep-rooted traditions, history, and passion for life. Throughout the year, a wide variety of festivals take place in every region, offering visitors a chance to experience Italy's unique customs, whether in the form of historical reenactments, religious celebrations, or artistic festivals.

Carnival (Venice)

One of the most famous festivals in Italy is Carnival, particularly in Venice, where the city transforms into a spectacular display of costumes and masks. Carnival is celebrated in the weeks leading up to Lent, with origins dating back to the Middle Ages. During this time, Venetians and visitors alike don elaborate, historically inspired costumes and participate in masquerade balls, parades, and performances throughout the city. The streets are filled with music, and the iconic Venetian masks add a sense of mystery and excitement to the festivities.

Palio di Siena (Siena)

The Palio di Siena is one of the most famous and historic horse races in the world, held twice a year (in July and August) in the Piazza del Campo of Siena. The race is fiercely contested by riders representing different districts (contrade) of the city, and the event is steeped in tradition and pageantry. The Palio is more than just a race; it's a celebration of Siena's history and pride, with parades, flag-throwing displays, and medieval costumes adding to the spectacle.

Festa di San Giovanni (Florence and Genoa)

Celebrating the patron saint of Florence and Genoa, Festa di San Giovanni is a major event in both cities, taking place on June 24. In Florence, the day is marked by historical parades, fireworks, and the traditional sport of Calcio Storico, a rough and competitive combination of soccer, rugby, and wrestling played in period costumes. Genoa celebrates with religious processions, cultural performances, and feasts, all in honor of their beloved saint.

Umbria Jazz Festival (Perugia)

For music lovers, the Umbria Jazz Festival in Perugia is one of Italy's top cultural events. Held every July, this internationally renowned festival attracts some of the world's greatest jazz musicians, along with tens of thousands of fans. The festival combines stunning venues with exceptional performances, creating an unforgettable atmosphere for music enthusiasts.

Religious Festivals

Italy is home to many religious festivals, each reflecting the country's deep Catholic roots. Easter celebrations, particularly in Rome, are a major event, with the Pope's Mass at St. Peter's Basilica drawing thousands of pilgrims. Other important religious festivals include La Festa della Madonna della Salute in Venice and the Feast of Saint Agatha in Catania, which feature processions, prayers, and feasting.

Local Arts and Music

Italy has long been a leader in the arts, from painting and sculpture to opera and contemporary music. The country's contributions to Western art and music are immeasurable, and its cities remain hubs for artists and musicians alike.

Visual Arts

Italy's influence on the world of art cannot be overstated. As the birthplace of the Renaissance, the country produced some of the greatest artists in history, including Michelangelo, Leonardo da Vinci, Raphael, Caravaggio, and Titian. These artists' works can be seen in Italy's museums, churches, and public spaces, with masterpieces such as The Last Supper in Milan, The Sistine Chapel in Vatican City, and The School of Athens in the Vatican Museums drawing millions of visitors.

In addition to its historic contributions, Italy remains an important center for contemporary art. Cities like Venice host international art exhibitions, including the prestigious Venice Biennale, which showcases cutting-edge contemporary art from around the world.

Opera and Classical Music

Italy is the birthplace of opera, and its rich tradition of classical music continues to thrive today. La Scala in Milan, one of the world's most famous opera houses, has hosted performances by legendary composers like Verdi and Puccini. Opera enthusiasts can also attend performances in other historic venues like Teatro San Carlo in Naples and Teatro La Fenice in Venice.

Beyond opera, Italy has produced numerous renowned composers and conductors, contributing to both classical and modern music. Italy also boasts a lively music scene that includes everything from traditional folk music to contemporary pop and jazz.

Film and Cinema

Italian cinema has had a profound impact on the world of film, from the Neorealism movement of the 1940s and 1950s—led by directors like Roberto Rossellini, Vittorio De Sica, and Federico Fellini—to contemporary filmmakers who continue to push the boundaries of storytelling

CHAPTER 6: ADVENTURE AND RECREATION

Credit@google

Italy offers an abundance of opportunities for adventure and outdoor recreation, from its rugged mountains and lush national parks to its picturesque coastlines and serene lakes. Whether you're looking for thrilling outdoor activities or relaxing boat tours, Italy has something for every type of adventurer. This chapter explores the best of Italy's parks and outdoor activities, water sports and boat tours, and exciting day trips you can take from various parts of the country.

Parks and Outdoor Activities

Italy's diverse landscapes provide an ideal setting for outdoor enthusiasts. From the towering peaks of the Alps to the scenic trails of the Apennines, the country's national parks and natural reserves offer endless opportunities for hiking, biking, and exploring.

Cinque Terre National Park

Located along the Ligurian coast, Cinque Terre National Park is renowned for its breathtaking coastal scenery and charming villages. The park encompasses five picturesque towns—Monterosso al Mare, Vernazza, Corniglia, Manarola, and Riomaggiore—connected by scenic hiking trails. The Sentiero Azzurro (Blue Trail) offers spectacular views of the rugged coastline and the turquoise waters of the Mediterranean. The park is also a great destination for rock climbing and bird watching.

Dolomiti di Sesto Nature Park

In the northeastern part of Italy, Dolomiti di Sesto Nature Park showcases the stunning landscape of the Dolomite Mountains. This park is known for its dramatic rock formations, alpine meadows, and diverse wildlife. Outdoor activities here include hiking, climbing, and skiing in the winter months. The Tre Cime di Lavaredo (Three Peaks) area is particularly popular for its spectacular hiking trails and panoramic views.

Gran Paradiso National Park

Established in 1922, Gran Paradiso National Park is Italy's oldest national park and is located in the Aosta Valley and Piedmont regions. The park is home to a wide range of flora and fauna, including the elusive ibex and chamois. Visitors can enjoy hiking, wildlife spotting, and mountaineering. The park's rugged terrain and high-altitude lakes make it a favorite among serious hikers and nature lovers.

Val Grande National Park

Val Grande National Park, situated in the Piedmont region, offers a more remote and rugged wilderness experience. Known for its dramatic landscapes, dense forests, and steep valleys, this park is ideal for those seeking solitude and adventure. Hiking trails wind through the park, providing opportunities for exploring its remote beauty and enjoying the serene environment.

Lake Como

Lake Como, located in the Lombardy region, is renowned for its stunning scenery and outdoor activities. The lake's picturesque surroundings offer opportunities for hiking, with trails providing panoramic views of the lake and surrounding mountains. Visitors can also enjoy water sports like kayaking and sailing, or simply relax along the lake's charming promenades.

Water Sports and Boat Tours

Italy's extensive coastline, lakes, and rivers provide ample opportunities for water-based activities. Whether you're interested in exploring the coast by boat, diving into crystal-clear waters, or enjoying a leisurely gondola ride, Italy's water activities offer something for everyone.

Sailing and Boating

Italy's coastlines, particularly along the Amalfi Coast, the Italian Riviera, and the islands of Sicily and Sardinia, are perfect for sailing and boating. You can rent a boat or join a sailing tour to explore secluded coves, hidden beaches, and charming coastal towns. The Sardinian archipelago is especially renowned for its beautiful sailing routes and crystal-clear waters.

Gondola Rides in Venice

A quintessential Venetian experience is a gondola ride through the city's intricate canal system. Glide through the winding canals, admire the unique architecture of Venice's buildings, and enjoy the romantic ambiance of this historic city. Gondola rides are available throughout the day and evening, providing a unique perspective on Venice's beauty.

Snorkeling and Scuba Diving

Italy's coastal waters are teeming with marine life, making them ideal for snorkeling and scuba diving. The Blue Grotto on the island of Capri and the underwater park of Porto Conte in Sardinia are popular spots for exploring vibrant marine ecosystems. The Egadi Islands and the Aeolian Islands also offer excellent diving opportunities, with clear waters and diverse sea life.

Kayaking and Stand-Up Paddleboarding

For a more active water experience, kayaking and stand-up paddleboarding (SUP) are great ways to explore Italy's lakes and coastlines. The serene waters of Lake Garda and the coastal areas of Cinque Terre are ideal for these activities. Paddle along the coastline, discover hidden beaches, and enjoy the tranquility of Italy's natural beauty.

River Rafting

In regions with fast-flowing rivers, such as the Valley of the Noce River in Trentino-Alto Adige, river rafting is a thrilling adventure. Navigate through rapids, enjoy the adrenaline rush, and take in the stunning alpine scenery. River rafting is a great way to combine adventure with the natural beauty of Italy's mountainous regions.

Day Trips from Italy

Italy's central location in Europe makes it a great starting point for day trips to neighboring countries and nearby attractions. Whether you're interested in exploring historic cities, relaxing in scenic towns, or indulging in local cuisine, these day trips offer a range of experiences just a short distance from Italy's borders.

Day Trip to Switzerland

Switzerland's stunning landscapes and charming cities are easily accessible from northern Italy. A popular day trip destination is Lugano, a picturesque city located in the Italian-speaking region of Switzerland. Lugano offers beautiful lakeside views, outdoor activities, and a taste of Swiss culture. Alternatively, you can visit Zermatt and take a cable car up to the Matterhorn for spectacular alpine scenery.

Day Trip to France

From northern Italy, a day trip to Nice or Côte d'Azur in France is a fantastic way to experience the French Riviera. Enjoy the glamorous beaches, stroll along the Promenade des Anglais, and savor French cuisine in charming cafes. For a taste of French history and culture, you can also visit the city of Avignon, known for its medieval architecture and historical significance.

Day Trip to Slovenia

Ljubljana, the capital of Slovenia, is a charming and picturesque city located just a short drive from northern Italy. Explore the city's historic center, visit the impressive Ljubljana Castle, and enjoy the vibrant local culture. The nearby Lake Bled, with its stunning scenery and iconic island church, is another must-see destination.

Day Trip to Vatican City

For those staying in Rome, a day trip to Vatican City offers an in-depth exploration of one of the world's smallest independent states. Visit St. Peter's Basilica, the Vatican Museums, and the Sistine Chapel to experience the rich artistic and religious heritage of the Catholic Church.

Day Trip to Florence

Florence, the cradle of the Renaissance, is just a short train ride away from Rome and offers a wealth of historical and cultural attractions. Visit the Uffizi Gallery, admire Michelangelo's David, and explore the stunning architecture of the Duomo. Florence's charming streets and vibrant art scene make it an ideal day trip destination for art lovers and history enthusiasts.

CHAPTER 7: SHOPPING IN ITALY

Credit@google

Italy is renowned for its fashion, luxury goods, and unique artisanal products. From high-end boutiques in Milan to charming local markets in small towns, the country offers a diverse shopping experience. This chapter explores popular shopping districts, local crafts and souvenirs, and provides valuable shopping tips and tricks to help you navigate Italy's retail landscape.

Popular Shopping Districts

Italy's cities are treasure troves for shoppers, each offering its own distinctive shopping experience. Whether you're looking for high fashion, luxury goods, or unique local items, these shopping districts are must-visit destinations.

Milan's Fashion District

Milan is synonymous with high fashion and luxury shopping. The city's Quadrilatero d'Oro (Golden Rectangle) is the epicenter of Milan's fashion scene. This upscale district is bordered by Via Montenapoleone, Via della Spiga, Via Manzoni, and Via Sant'Andrea. Here, you'll find flagship stores of luxury brands such as Gucci, Prada, Versace, and Armani. Milan's fashion district is perfect for those seeking the latest trends and designer pieces.

Rome's Via del Corso and Via Condotti

In Rome, Via del Corso is a major shopping street offering a mix of international brands and Italian stores. It's ideal for those looking to explore popular chain stores and mid-range fashion. For high-end shopping, Via Condotti is Rome's luxury shopping street, home to prestigious boutiques including Louis Vuitton, Chanel, and Dior. The area around Piazza di Spagna is also known for its elegant shops and boutiques.

Florence's Via de' Tornabuoni

Florence is famous for its art and history, but it also offers excellent shopping opportunities. Via de' Tornabuoni is the city's luxury shopping street, lined with boutiques from renowned fashion houses such as Salvatore Ferragamo and Gucci, which originated in Florence. The street is perfect for those looking to invest in high-quality Italian fashion and accessories.

Venice's Rialto Market

For a more traditional shopping experience, Venice's Rialto Market is a vibrant and historic marketplace located near the Rialto Bridge. Here, you'll find an array of fresh produce, seafood, and local specialties. The market is also a great place to purchase Venetian crafts and souvenirs, such as Murano glass and Burano lace.

Turin's Via Roma and Via Lagrange

In Turin, Via Roma and Via Lagrange are the main shopping streets offering a blend of high-end stores, international brands, and local boutiques. Via Roma features luxury retailers, while Via Lagrange provides a more eclectic mix of fashion, accessories, and specialty shops.

Local Crafts and Souvenirs

Italy is renowned for its artisanal craftsmanship and unique souvenirs. Each region has its own specialties, offering a wide range of handcrafted items and traditional goods.

Murano Glass

Murano, a small island near Venice, is famous for its exquisite glasswork. Murano glass is renowned for its vibrant colors and intricate designs. Visitors can purchase a variety of items, from delicate glass jewelry to elaborate sculptures and chandeliers. Make sure to buy from reputable stores to ensure authenticity.

Florentine Leather Goods

Florence is known for its high-quality leather products. From handbags and wallets to jackets and shoes, Florentine leather goods are crafted with precision and skill. The San Lorenzo Market is a popular spot to find leather items, as well as other local products like handmade paper and jewelry.

Ceramics from Deruta

Deruta, located in Umbria, is famous for its colorful ceramics. Traditional Deruta ceramics feature intricate patterns and vibrant colors, making them a perfect souvenir. Items range from decorative plates and bowls to tiles and vases. Look for shops that offer traditional designs as well as contemporary interpretations.

Burano Lace

Burano, another island near Venice, is renowned for its intricate lacework. Burano lace is handcrafted using traditional techniques passed down through generations. Lace items, such as tablecloths, napkins, and clothing, are delicate and beautifully crafted. Purchasing from local artisans ensures that you get authentic Burano lace.

Tuscan Wine and Olive Oil

The Tuscan region is famous for its wine and olive oil. Chianti wines, Brunello di Montalcino, and Vernaccia di San Gimignano are highly regarded. Extra virgin olive oil from Tuscany is known for its rich flavor and quality. Local markets and specialized stores in Tuscany offer a variety of wines and olive oils that make great gifts or personal keepsakes.

Shopping Tips and Tricks

Navigating Italy's shopping scene can be both exciting and overwhelming. Here are some tips and tricks to help you make the most of your shopping experience:

1. *Know the Sales Seasons*

Italy has two main sales seasons: summer (July-August) and winter (January-February). During these periods, you can find significant discounts on fashion, accessories, and other items. Sales usually start in mid-January and mid-July, but the exact dates can vary by region and store.

2. *Shop at Local Markets*

Local markets are great places to find unique and authentic items, often at more reasonable prices than in high-end boutiques. Markets offer a chance to interact with local vendors, discover regional specialties, and enjoy a more immersive shopping experience.

3. *Be Aware of VAT Refunds*

As a non-EU resident, you are eligible for a VAT (Value Added Tax) refund on purchases made in Italy. To qualify, you must spend over a certain amount (usually €154.94) in a single store. Ask for a VAT refund form when making your purchase and keep your receipts. At the airport, present your form and receipts to customs to receive your refund.

4. *Bargain Wisely*

While bargaining is not common in most retail stores, it is acceptable in some local markets and smaller shops. Approach bargaining with respect and politeness. In high-end boutiques, prices are usually fixed, and bargaining is not typically practiced.

5. *Check for Authenticity*

When purchasing luxury goods or local crafts, ensure that you are buying from reputable stores or authorized dealers to guarantee authenticity. Look for certificates of authenticity or provenance for high-value items, such as Murano glass or designer fashion.

6. *Learn Basic Italian Phrases*

Knowing a few basic Italian phrases can enhance your shopping experience. Simple phrases such as "Quanto costa?" (How much does it cost?) and "Posso pagare con carta di credito?" (Can I pay with a credit card?) can be very helpful.

7. *Explore Small Boutiques*

While major shopping districts offer high-end brands, don't overlook small boutiques and artisanal shops. These smaller stores often carry unique, handcrafted items and provide a more personalized shopping experience.

8. *Enjoy the Experience*

Shopping in Italy is not just about purchasing items; it's about enjoying the experience. Take your time to explore different stores, interact with local vendors, and appreciate the craftsmanship and artistry behind the products you find.

Italy's shopping scene is as diverse and dynamic as its culture and history. From luxury fashion in Milan to local crafts in Venice, there is something for every shopper. Whether you're looking for high-end fashion, unique souvenirs, or traditional artisanal goods, Italy offers an enriching and memorable shopping experience.

CHAPTER 8: NIGHTLIFE AND ENTERTAINMENT

Credit@google

Italy's vibrant nightlife scene is as varied as its cultural heritage, offering something for everyone from chic cocktail bars to lively nightclubs, and from classical music performances to unique night tours. Whether you're looking to dance the night away, enjoy live music, or explore a city's after-dark charm, Italy has an exciting range of options. This chapter delves into the best bars and clubs, live music and performances, and night tours and experiences to help you make the most of Italy's nightlife.

Best Bars and Clubs

Italy's cities boast a diverse array of bars and clubs, catering to all tastes and styles. From sophisticated cocktail lounges to high-energy nightclubs, there's something for every type of night owl.

Milan's Trendy Hotspots

Milan, known as a fashion and design capital, also has a thriving nightlife scene. Navigli District is famous for its vibrant bar scene, with an array of cocktail bars and casual hangouts lining the canals. Rita & Cocktails is a popular spot known for its inventive cocktails and lively atmosphere. For a more upscale experience, Nottingham Forest offers a creative cocktail menu in a chic setting.

If you're into dancing, Hollywood Milano is a high-energy nightclub with international DJs and a stylish crowd. The Club and Alcatraz are also well-regarded venues offering a mix of live music and DJ sets.

Rome's Classic and Contemporary Venues

In Rome, the Trastevere neighborhood is a hotspot for nightlife, featuring a range of bars and pubs. Bar San Calisto is a beloved local favorite with a relaxed vibe and affordable drinks. For a more sophisticated experience, Freni e Frizioni offers creative cocktails and a chic atmosphere.

When it comes to nightclubs, Shari Vari Playhouse is a stylish venue with an eclectic mix of music and a glamorous crowd. Piper Club, one of Rome's historic nightclubs, has been a mainstay in the city's nightlife since the 1960s and continues to offer a lively mix of music and entertainment.

Florence's Lively Nightlife

Florence is known for its vibrant and diverse nightlife. Red Garter is a popular American-style bar offering karaoke nights and a lively atmosphere. For a more elegant night out, The Fusion Bar offers a sophisticated cocktail menu in a stylish setting.

Central Park is a must-visit nightclub in Florence, featuring international DJs and a high-energy dance floor. Tenax is another renowned club that offers an impressive lineup of DJs and a cutting-edge music scene.

Venice's Unique Night Spots

Venice offers a more relaxed but charming nightlife experience. Harry's Bar, a historic venue famous for inventing the Bellini cocktail, provides a classic Venetian bar experience. For a more casual setting, Al Timon offers a laid-back atmosphere with great drinks and views of the canals.

Nightlife in Venice also includes Teatro La Fenice, where you can enjoy classical music and opera in one of Italy's most renowned theaters.

Live Music and Performances

Italy's rich cultural heritage is reflected in its vibrant live music scene, which ranges from classical concerts to contemporary performances. The country is also home to numerous theaters and performance venues showcasing a wide variety of artistic expressions.

Opera and Classical Music

Italy is synonymous with opera, and cities like Milan, Rome, and Venice are home to some of the world's most prestigious opera houses. La Scala in Milan is one of the most famous opera houses globally, renowned for its grand productions and exceptional acoustics. Teatro dell'Opera di Roma offers a range of opera and classical music performances, while Teatro La Fenice in Venice is celebrated for its stunning performances and historic significance.

Jazz and Contemporary Music

Rome's Casa del Jazz and Milan's Blue Note are top venues for jazz enthusiasts. Casa del Jazz offers a relaxed atmosphere and a diverse lineup of jazz performances, while Blue Note Milan features international jazz artists and an intimate setting.

In Florence, Jazz Club Firenze provides a cozy venue for enjoying live jazz performances. For contemporary music, Viper Theatre in Florence hosts a variety of live performances, including rock and electronic music.

Theater and Performing Arts

Italy's theatrical tradition is vibrant and diverse. Teatro Piccolo in Milan offers a range of contemporary plays and performances, while Teatro Stabile in Rome is known for its classic and modern theatrical productions. Teatro Metastasio in Prato is another prominent theater offering a mix of classical and modern performances.

Venice also offers unique theatrical experiences, such as the Carnevale di Venezia (Venetian Carnival), which features elaborate costumes, masquerades, and theatrical performances throughout the city.

Night Tours and Experiences

Exploring a city by night can provide a different perspective and uncover hidden gems. Night tours and unique experiences offer an opportunity to see Italy's cities in a new light.

Rome by Night

Rome's night tours provide a captivating look at the city's historic landmarks illuminated after dark.

The Rome Night Tour includes visits to the Colosseum, Roman Forum, and Pantheon, all beautifully lit at night. For a more immersive experience, consider a guided walking tour that explores Rome's charming neighborhoods and hidden spots.

Venice Gondola Night Tours

A gondola ride through the canals of Venice is a classic experience, and a night ride offers a magical view of the city's illuminated architecture. Gondola tours provide a romantic and tranquil way to explore the canals and see Venice from a unique perspective.

Florence's Illuminated Walking Tours

Florence's walking tours offer a chance to explore the city's landmarks and historic sites under the evening sky. The Florence Night Tour includes visits to the Piazza della Signoria, Ponte Vecchio, and other iconic sites, providing insights into the city's history and architecture.

Milan's Nightlife Cruises

In Milan, consider taking a night cruise along the city's canals. The cruise provides a relaxing way to enjoy the evening scenery and see the city's vibrant nightlife from the water. Some tours include dinner and drinks, making for a memorable night out.

Turin's Nighttime Cultural Tours

Turin offers unique cultural experiences after dark. The Turin Night Tour includes visits to landmarks such as the Mole Antonelliana and Piazza Castello, and some tours feature stops at local cafes and bars. Turin is also known for its mysterious and haunted tours, exploring the city's hidden legends and folklore.

CHAPTER 9: TRANSPORTATION WITHIN ITALY

Credit@google

Italy's diverse landscapes and historic cities offer a range of transportation options, each suited to different needs and preferences. From efficient public transit systems to bike and scooter rentals, and practical tips for navigating urban areas, understanding your options can enhance your travel experience. This chapter provides a comprehensive guide to Italy's transportation infrastructure, including the public transit system, bike and scooter rentals, and essential tips for navigating cities.

Public Transit System

Italy boasts a well-developed public transit system that includes trains, buses, trams, and metro services. Each mode of transportation offers distinct advantages, depending on your travel needs and destinations.

1. *Trains*

Italy's train network is extensive and connects major cities, regions, and even neighboring countries. The Italian State Railways, Trenitalia, operates most of the train services, including regional, intercity, and high-speed trains.

- High-Speed Trains: Italy's high-speed trains, Frecciarossa and Frecciargento, offer fast and comfortable travel between major cities like Milan, Rome, Florence, and Naples. These trains can reach speeds of up to 300 km/h (186 mph), significantly reducing travel times. Italo is another high-speed service, providing competitive options on similar routes.

- Intercity Trains: For travel between cities that are not on the high-speed network, Intercity and Intercity Notte (night trains) provide comfortable options. These trains offer amenities such as air conditioning, power outlets, and dining services.

- Regional Trains: Regionale trains serve local routes and are ideal for exploring smaller towns and rural areas. While slower than high-speed trains, they provide an economical way to travel and are well-suited for short to medium distances.

- Tickets and Passes: Tickets for Trenitalia can be purchased online, at train stations, or via mobile apps. Booking in advance often secures better prices, especially for high-speed trains. Consider purchasing a Eurail Pass or Interrail Pass if you plan to travel extensively by train across Italy and Europe.

2. *Buses*

Italy's bus system complements the train network, offering connections to areas not served by rail. Several companies operate regional and long-distance bus services:

- Regional Buses: Local bus services within cities and towns are managed by various regional companies. In larger cities like Rome and Milan, buses are an integral part of the public transit system, providing extensive coverage.

- Long-Distance Buses: Companies such as FlixBus and MarinoBus offer long-distance routes connecting major cities and towns. These buses are often more economical than trains and provide amenities such as Wi-Fi and power outlets.

- Tickets and Schedules: Bus tickets can be purchased at stations, online, or through mobile apps. Schedules vary by route and company, so check timetables in advance and be prepared for potential delays, especially on regional routes.

3. *Trams*

Trams are a popular mode of transportation in several Italian cities, including Milan, Rome, and Turin:

- Milan: The tram network in Milan is extensive, covering the city and its suburbs. Tram lines 1, 3, 5, 7, and 9 are among the most frequently used, connecting key areas such as the city center, the university district, and residential neighborhoods.

- Rome: Rome's tram system includes several lines that serve different parts of the city. Tram lines 3 and 8 are particularly notable for connecting popular destinations, including Trastevere and the historic center.

- Turin: The tram network in Turin includes several lines that provide access to key areas of the city, such as the Porta Nuova and Porta Susa train stations.

- Tickets: Tram tickets are often integrated with bus and metro tickets, allowing for seamless transfers. Validate your ticket before boarding to avoid fines.

4. *Metro*

The metro systems in major cities offer a quick and efficient way to navigate urban areas:

- Milan: Milan's metro system consists of four lines (M1, M2, M3, M5) that cover key areas of the city.

The metro is known for its punctuality and cleanliness.

- Rome: Rome's metro includes three lines (A, B, C) that connect various parts of the city. Line A runs from the Battistini district to Anagnina, while Line B connects Laurentina to Rebibbia. Line C serves the eastern parts of Rome.

- Naples: The Naples metro consists of several lines, with Line 1 being the primary route connecting the city center to the northern suburbs.

- Tickets: Metro tickets can be purchased at stations or via mobile apps. They are usually valid for a certain duration, allowing for unlimited travel within the time frame.

5. *Ferries*

In coastal cities and islands, ferries provide a scenic and practical means of transportation:

- Venice: The Vaporetto (water bus) system in Venice serves as the primary public transport method, connecting the islands and main points in the city. Line 1 is the most popular, running along the Grand Canal.

- Naples and Amalfi Coast: Ferries connect Naples with the islands of Capri, Ischia, and Procida. The

Amalfi Coast also has ferry services that link towns such as Amalfi, Positano, and Sorrento.

- Tickets: Ferry tickets can be purchased at ticket offices, online, or via mobile apps. Some ferries offer passes for unlimited travel within a certain period.

Bike and Scooter Rentals

Renting bikes and scooters is a convenient and enjoyable way to explore Italy's cities and countryside. Many cities offer rental services that cater to both casual tourists and avid cyclists.

1. *Bike Rentals*

- City Bikes: In cities like Milan, Florence, and Rome, bike rentals are a popular option for getting around. Companies such as BikeMi in Milan, CitiBike in Florence, and Roma Bike in Rome offer various types of bikes, including city bikes, e-bikes, and mountain bikes.

- Touring Bikes: For those looking to explore Italy's scenic countryside, many rental shops offer touring bikes. These bikes are designed for longer distances and can handle diverse terrain. Cycling tours are available in regions such as Tuscany, the Dolomites, and the Italian Alps.

- Bike Paths and Trails: Italy has numerous bike paths and trails, including the Ciclovia Alpe Adria in the Alps and the Ciclovia del Sole in Tuscany. These routes offer picturesque views and are suitable for both leisurely rides and more challenging cycling adventures.

- Rental Services: Bike rentals can be arranged through local shops or online platforms. Rental rates typically vary based on the type of bike and rental duration. Many cities also offer bike-sharing schemes, where you can pick up and drop off bikes at various stations.

2. *Scooter Rentals*

- Electric Scooters: Electric scooters have become increasingly popular in Italian cities due to their convenience and eco-friendliness. Companies like Lime, Bird, and Circ operate in cities such as Milan, Rome, and Florence. These scooters are ideal for short trips and can be rented via mobile apps.

- Motor Scooters: For longer trips or to cover more distance, renting a motor scooter is a great option. Companies such as Scooterino and Bobby offer motor scooters in various cities. These scooters are typically available in 50cc and 125cc models, with the latter requiring a valid motorcycle license.

- Rental Requirements: To rent a motor scooter, you'll need a valid motorcycle license and may be required to provide a deposit. Electric scooters usually require a valid ID and a credit card for payment. Helmets are provided with most rentals and are mandatory for safety.

- Safety and Regulations: When renting bikes or scooters, familiarize yourself with local traffic laws and safety regulations. Wear a helmet, follow traffic signals, and be cautious of pedestrians and other vehicles. Many cities have dedicated bike lanes and scooter zones, making navigation easier and safer.

Tips for Navigating Cities

Navigating Italian cities can be both exciting and challenging due to their historical layouts and bustling streets. Here are some tips to help you move around with ease:

1. *Understand City Layouts*

- Historic Centers: Many Italian cities have historic centers with narrow, winding streets. Familiarize yourself with the layout of the city and identify key landmarks to help with orientation. Maps and GPS apps can be invaluable for navigating these areas.

- Public Transit Maps: Obtain maps of public transit systems, including buses, trams, and metro lines. Most cities provide these maps at transit stations or online. Understanding the routes and connections will help you plan your journeys more efficiently.

2. *Plan Your Routes*

- Use Navigation Apps: Apps like Google Maps and Citymapper offer real-time navigation and public transit information. These apps can help you find the best routes and estimated travel times.

- Check Schedules: Public transit schedules can vary, especially during holidays or weekends. Check the schedules in advance and allow extra time for potential delays.

- Plan for Traffic: In major cities, traffic congestion can impact travel times. Plan for additional time during peak hours and consider using public transit or biking to avoid traffic jams.

3. *Be Aware of Local Customs*

- Tipping: Tipping is not always expected in Italy, but rounding up the fare or leaving small change in taxis and at restaurants is appreciated. For public transportation, tips are generally not required, but showing gratitude to drivers or staff can be a nice gesture.

- Language: While many Italians in tourist areas speak English, learning a few basic Italian phrases can be helpful. Phrases like "Dove si trova la fermata dell'autobus?" (Where is the bus stop?) or "Quanto costa un biglietto?" (How much is a ticket?) can assist in navigating public transit and interactions with locals.

4. *Understand Payment and Ticketing Systems*

- Purchase Tickets in Advance: For trains, buses, and metro services, purchasing tickets in advance can save time and often provide cost savings. Online booking is available for many services, allowing you to secure seats and manage travel plans more easily.

- Validate Your Ticket: In many Italian cities, especially for buses and trams, tickets need to be validated before boarding. Look for validation machines at stations or on board to avoid fines.

- Passes and Cards: Consider purchasing city travel passes or cards if you plan to use public transit frequently. For example, Rome offers the Roma Pass, which provides unlimited access to public transit and discounts on attractions.

5. *Safety and Etiquette*

- Stay Aware of Your Surroundings: Public transit and popular tourist areas can attract pickpockets. Keep your belongings secure and be vigilant, especially in crowded areas.

- Respect Local Etiquette: On public transportation, it's customary to give up seats to the elderly, pregnant women, and individuals with disabilities. Maintain a respectful volume and avoid disruptive behavior.

- Use Bike Lanes: When biking in cities, use designated bike lanes where available. Adhere to traffic rules and be cautious of pedestrians and vehicles. Ensure your bike is securely locked when not in use.

6. *Emergency Services and Assistance*

- Emergency Numbers: Familiarize yourself with local emergency numbers. In Italy, the general emergency number is 112 for police, medical, and fire services.

- Assistance and Information: Most cities have tourist information centers where you can get help with transportation queries, maps, and other travel-related assistance. These centers are often located at major train stations or central tourist areas.

7. *Accessibility Considerations*

- Accessible Transport: Major cities like Rome and Milan are improving accessibility in their public transit systems, but not all stations and vehicles are fully accessible. Check in advance if you have specific accessibility needs and look for services like accessible taxis or special assistance at train stations.

- Travel with Disabilities: For those with mobility impairments, Italy offers various services, such as accessible public transit options and assistance at airports and train stations. The Trenitalia website provides detailed information on accessibility features for train services.

8. *Local Transit Variations*

- City-Specific Information: Each Italian city has its own transit network and rules. For instance, Venice relies heavily on water transport, while cities like Rome and Milan have extensive metro systems.

Research local transit options before your visit to ensure a smooth travel experience.

- Regional Differences: In smaller towns and rural areas, public transportation may be less frequent. Renting a car or using taxis might be more practical for reaching remote destinations.

Navigating Italy's transportation options effectively requires an understanding of the various systems available and how to use them efficiently. By familiarizing yourself with the public transit system, utilizing bike and scooter rentals, and following practical tips for city navigation, you can enhance your travel experience and make the most of your time in Italy. Whether you're exploring bustling cities or serene countryside, Italy's transportation infrastructure provides the tools you need to discover its rich cultural and historical treasures.

CHAPTER 10: PRACTICAL INFORMATION

When traveling to Italy, having practical information at your fingertips can make your trip smoother and more enjoyable. This chapter covers essential details on currency, banking, and ATMs, health and safety tips, and useful apps and resources to help you navigate your Italian adventure with confidence.

Currency, Banking, and ATMs

Understanding Italy's currency and banking system is crucial for managing your finances effectively while traveling.

1. **Currency**

Italy, as a member of the Eurozone, uses the Euro (€) as its official currency. The Euro is divided into 100 cents and comes in both coins and banknotes. The notes are available in denominations of €5, €10, €20, €50, €100, €200, and €500, while the coins come in €1, €2, 1 cent, 2 cents, 5 cents, 10 cents, 20 cents, and 50 cents.

- Currency Exchange: Currency exchange services are widely available throughout Italy. You can exchange your money at banks, exchange offices, and some hotels. Airports and train stations also have currency exchange counters. It's advisable to check the exchange rates and fees beforehand to ensure you get the best deal.

- Credit and Debit Cards: Major credit and debit cards (Visa, MasterCard, American Express) are widely accepted in Italy. You can use them for most transactions, including hotel stays, restaurant bills, and shopping. However, some smaller establishments or markets may only accept cash.

- Cash Requirements: While credit cards are commonly used, having some cash on hand is useful for smaller purchases, local markets, and places that don't accept cards. It's also helpful to carry small denominations for ease of payment.

2. *Banking*

- Bank Services: Banks in Italy typically operate from 8:30 AM to 1:30 PM and 2:30 PM to 4:00 PM, Monday to Friday. Some banks may open on Saturday mornings, but this varies by location. Many banks have English-speaking staff, especially in tourist areas.

- Opening Hours: Note that banks are closed on public holidays, which may affect your ability to exchange currency or use banking services. Check local holidays in advance to plan accordingly.

- Bank Fees: Banks may charge fees for currency exchange or using ATMs with international cards. It's a good idea to inquire about fees and compare them with those of local currency exchange services.

3. *ATMs*

- Availability: ATMs are widely available throughout Italy, including at airports, train stations, banks, and in urban areas. They offer a convenient way to withdraw cash in Euros.

- Using ATMs: Most ATMs accept international credit and debit cards. Ensure your card has a

4-digit PIN, as some ATMs may not accept longer PINs. Be aware of the language options available on the ATM screen to select your preferred language.

- Fees and Limits: Check with your bank regarding international ATM fees and withdrawal limits. Some ATMs may impose their own fees, so look for those that are affiliated with your home bank or offer better rates.

- Security: Use ATMs in well-lit, secure areas and cover your PIN when entering it. Be cautious of any suspicious activity around the ATM, and if the machine retains your card, contact your bank immediately.

Health and Safety Tips

Ensuring your health and safety while traveling is essential for a worry-free trip. Italy is generally a safe destination, but being prepared and informed can help you avoid potential issues.

1. *Health Precautions*
- Travel Insurance: It's highly recommended to purchase travel insurance that covers health emergencies, trip cancellations, and lost belongings. Ensure your insurance policy includes coverage for medical expenses abroad.

- Vaccinations and Health Requirements: Italy does not require specific vaccinations for entry, but make sure your routine vaccinations are up to date. If you're traveling from certain countries, you might need a yellow fever vaccination certificate.

- Healthcare Services: Italy has a high standard of healthcare, with public and private hospitals and clinics available. Emergency services are accessible via the number 118. EU citizens can use their European Health Insurance Card (EHIC) for state-provided healthcare services, while non-EU travelers should rely on their travel insurance.

- Medications: Carry any prescribed medications with you and bring a copy of the prescription in case you need to refill them. Some medications available over-the-counter in other countries might require a prescription in Italy.

- Food and Water: Tap water is generally safe to drink in Italy, but if you have concerns, bottled water is widely available. Be cautious with street food and ensure it's from reputable vendors to avoid foodborne illnesses.

2. *Safety Tips*

- General Safety: Italy is generally safe for tourists, but always stay alert and be aware of your surroundings, especially in crowded areas. Petty crimes like pickpocketing can occur, particularly in major cities and tourist hotspots.

- Emergency Numbers: Familiarize yourself with local emergency numbers: 112 for general emergencies, 113 for police, 118 for medical emergencies, and 115 for fire services.

- Local Laws and Regulations: Adhere to local laws and regulations, including traffic rules, alcohol consumption laws, and any specific rules related to areas you visit. Respect cultural norms and practices to avoid misunderstandings.

- Safety in Cities: In cities, avoid walking alone late at night in poorly lit areas and be cautious when using ATMs. Use reputable transportation options and be aware of common scams targeting tourists.

- Natural Disasters: Italy is prone to natural disasters such as earthquakes and floods. Familiarize yourself with safety procedures in case of an emergency and follow local advisories.

3. *Personal Safety*

- Emergency Contacts: Keep a list of emergency contacts, including local authorities, your country's embassy or consulate, and your insurance provider. Share your travel itinerary with family or friends for added safety.

- Lost or Stolen Documents: In case of lost or stolen passports, report it to the local police and your country's embassy or consulate immediately. They can assist with emergency travel documents and guide you through the process.

Useful Apps and Resources

Leveraging technology can significantly enhance your travel experience in Italy. Here are some essential apps and resources to help you navigate the country more effectively.

1. *Navigation and Transport Apps*

- Google Maps: Provides detailed maps, directions, and real-time traffic information. It's useful for navigating cities, finding attractions, and getting public transit directions.

- Citymapper: Offers comprehensive public transit information for major cities, including route planning, schedules, and fare details.

- Rome2rio: Helps you find and compare different transportation options between destinations, including trains, buses, ferries, and flights.

- Moovit: Provides public transit information, including real-time updates and route planning, for various cities across Italy.

2. ***Language and Communication Apps***

- Google Translate: Useful for translating text and speech between languages. It can help with reading menus, signs, and communicating with locals.

- Duolingo: A language learning app that can help you pick up basic Italian phrases and vocabulary before and during your trip.

3. ***Currency and Banking Apps***

- XE Currency: Provides real-time currency exchange rates and allows you to convert prices and track spending.

- Revolut: A financial app that offers currency exchange, budgeting tools, and a travel-friendly debit card with no foreign transaction fees.

4. *Health and Safety Apps*

- TravelSmart: Offers travel insurance information, emergency contacts, and health advice specific to your destination.

- Emergency Services: Some countries have specific apps that provide emergency services and safety information. Check if your country has such an app and download it before your trip.

5. *Local Recommendations and Guides*

-    TripAdvisor: Provides reviews and recommendations for restaurants, attractions, and hotels, helping you make informed decisions.

- Yelp: Offers local business reviews and ratings, including restaurants, shops, and services.

- TheFork: A restaurant reservation app that offers reviews, discounts, and the ability to book tables at popular dining spots.

6. *General Travel Resources*

- Lonely Planet: Provides travel guides, tips, and recommendations for various destinations, including Italy.

- Rick Steves' Italy: Offers detailed travel advice, itineraries, and recommendations for exploring Italy.

Understanding practical aspects of traveling in Italy, from currency and banking to health and safety, and using relevant apps and resources, will ensure a smoother and more enjoyable experience. Being well-prepared helps you focus on enjoying your Italian adventure, exploring its rich culture, and making the most of your time in this beautiful country.

CHAPTER 11: LOCAL CUSTOMS AND ETIQUETTE

Credit@google

Italy is a country rich in culture, history, and tradition. Understanding and respecting local customs and etiquette will enhance your travel experience and help you navigate social interactions smoothly. This chapter provides insights into do's and don'ts, tipping and manners, and language basics to ensure you make a positive impression and enjoy your stay in Italy.

1. *Do's and Don'ts*

Do's

- Respect Local Traditions: Italy has a diverse cultural heritage with regional customs. Embrace local traditions, such as participating in festivals or local celebrations, and show respect for historical sites and landmarks.

- Dress Appropriately: Italians are known for their style and fashion sense. Dress neatly and elegantly, especially when visiting religious sites or dining at upscale restaurants. Avoid overly casual attire like shorts and flip-flops in such settings.

- Practice Politeness: Use polite greetings such as "Buongiorno" (Good morning) and "Buonasera" (Good evening) when interacting with locals. A friendly demeanor and respect for social norms go a long way.

- Queue Properly: Italians value orderly lines. Whether waiting for public transportation or at a café, make sure to join the end of the line and wait your turn.

- Be Punctual: While the pace of life in Italy may be relaxed, punctuality is appreciated, especially for business meetings or formal events. Arrive on time to show respect for others' schedules.

- Engage in Local Cuisine: Italian food is an integral part of the culture. Explore local specialties, enjoy traditional meals, and appreciate the regional variations in Italian cuisine.

Don'ts

- Avoid Loud Behavior: Italians generally speak in moderate tones, especially in public spaces like restaurants and public transportation. Avoid loud conversations or disruptive behavior that might disturb others.

- Don't Rush Your Meals: Dining in Italy is often a leisurely experience. Don't rush through meals or ask for the check immediately. Savor the food and enjoy the time spent at the table.

- Don't Overlook Table Manners: Observe local table manners, such as keeping your hands on the table (but not your elbows) and using utensils appropriately. Avoid starting your meal before everyone is served.

- Avoid Touching Artifacts: When visiting museums and historical sites, refrain from touching exhibits or artifacts. Respect signs and guidelines to preserve the integrity of these cultural treasures.

- Don't Expect Stores to Be Open All Day: Many shops and businesses close for a few hours in the afternoon for a break (riposo). Plan your shopping and errands around these hours.

- Don't Criticize Local Customs: Respect local customs, even if they differ from your own cultural practices. Avoid making negative comments about local traditions or ways of life.

2. *Tipping and Manners*

Tipping Practices

- Restaurants: In Italian restaurants, a service charge (servizio) is often included in the bill, particularly in tourist areas. However, it is customary to leave a small tip (around 5-10%) if the service is exceptional. Check your bill first to see if the service charge is included.

- Cafés and Bars: For a coffee or a drink at a café or bar, tipping is not obligatory but is appreciated. You can leave small change (a few coins) or round up the bill if you're pleased with the service.

- Taxis: Tipping taxi drivers is not required, but rounding up the fare or adding a small tip is a nice gesture, especially for good service or assistance with luggage.

- Hotels: In hotels, it's customary to leave a small tip for housekeeping (around €1-€2 per night) and for bellhops who assist with luggage. Tipping is generally not expected for reception staff, but it is appreciated for exceptional service.

- Guides and Tour Operators: If you're on a guided tour or participating in organized activities, tipping the guide or tour operator is appreciated if you're satisfied with their service. A tip of around 10-15% of the tour cost is standard.

Manners

- Greetings: Handshakes are common when meeting someone for the first time. In more familiar settings, Italians might greet each other with a kiss on both cheeks, starting with the right cheek.

- Polite Requests: Use "per favore" (please) and "grazie" (thank you) frequently when making requests or receiving services. Politeness is highly valued in Italian interactions.

- Addressing People: Use formal titles and last names when addressing someone you don't know well, such as "Signore" (Mr.) or "Signora" (Mrs.). With friends or people you know well, first names are appropriate.

- Respect Personal Space: While Italians may be more physically expressive, such as standing close during conversations, respect personal space and avoid standing too close to strangers.

- Handling Disputes: If a problem arises, address it calmly and politely. Italians appreciate direct but courteous communication when resolving issues.

Language Basics

While many Italians speak English, especially in tourist areas, learning a few basic Italian phrases can enhance your travel experience and show respect for the local culture.

Common Phrases

- *Greetings and Courtesies:*
  - Buongiorno (Good morning)
  - Buonasera (Good evening)
  - Buonanotte (Good night)
  - Arrivederci (Goodbye)
  - Per favore (Please)
  - Grazie (Thank you)

- Prego (You're welcome)

- *Introductions*:

  - Mi chiamo [Name] (My name is [Name])
  - Come si chiama? (What is your name?)

- *In Restaurants*:

  - Vorrei un tavolo per due, per favore (I'd like a table for two, please)
  - Il menù, per favore (The menu, please)
  - Quanto costa? (How much does it cost?)
  - Il conto, per favore (The check, please)

- *Asking for Directions*:

  - Dove si trova [place]? (Where is [place]?)

- Come posso arrivare a [place]? (How can I get to [place]?)

- C'è un bagno qui vicino? (Is there a bathroom nearby?)

- *Emergency Situations:*
  - Ho bisogno di aiuto (I need help)
  - Chiami un'ambulanza (Call an ambulance)
  - Dove si trova l'ospedale più vicino? (Where is the nearest hospital?)

Tips for Language Learning

- Practice Basic Phrases: Familiarize yourself with key phrases before traveling. Practice pronunciation and use language learning apps or resources to build confidence.

- Use Translation Apps: Apps like Google Translate can help bridge language gaps in real-time. They can translate text and speech, aiding in communication and understanding.

- Learn Local Dialects: In some regions, local dialects may differ from standard Italian. While not essential, learning a few regional terms or expressions can be appreciated by locals.

- Be Patient and Positive: Italians are generally understanding of language barriers and appreciate any effort to speak Italian. Approach conversations with a positive attitude and be patient if there are misunderstandings.

By adhering to local customs and etiquette, understanding tipping practices, and learning basic Italian phrases, you can navigate social interactions more effectively and enhance your overall travel experience in Italy. Embracing these cultural norms and showing respect for local traditions will help you connect with locals and enjoy your time in this beautiful country.

CHAPTER 12: SEASONAL CONSIDERATIONS

Credit@google

Italy's diverse climate and varied geography offer unique experiences throughout the year. Understanding the best times to visit, what to pack, and the weather conditions will help you plan your trip effectively and make the most of your Italian adventure. This chapter provides comprehensive guidance on these aspects to ensure you have a smooth and enjoyable stay.

Best Times to Visit

Italy's appeal spans all seasons, each offering distinct advantages. Your choice of travel time can significantly impact your experience.

Spring (March to May)

- Weather: Spring in Italy is characterized by mild temperatures and blooming landscapes. Daytime temperatures range from 15°C to 25°C (59°F to 77°F), with cooler evenings. Rain is occasional but generally light.

- Advantages: Spring is ideal for sightseeing and outdoor activities due to the pleasant weather. Tourist crowds are smaller compared to the summer months, making it a great time to explore major attractions and enjoy local festivals.

- Events: Key events include Easter celebrations, which vary in timing each year, and the Venice Biennale, a prominent art and architecture festival.

Many towns and cities also host flower festivals and outdoor markets.

Summer (June to August)

- Weather: Italian summers can be hot, with temperatures often exceeding 30°C (86°F) in most regions, particularly in southern Italy. Coastal areas and higher elevations offer some respite with milder temperatures.

- Advantages: Summer is perfect for enjoying Italy's beaches, outdoor festivals, and vibrant nightlife. Major cities are bustling with activity, and many cultural events and music festivals take place during this period.

- Events: Highlights include the Palio di Siena, a historic horse race held twice in July and August, and numerous outdoor concerts and theater performances. Coastal regions host beach festivals and water sports events.

Autumn (September to November)

- Weather: Autumn brings cooler temperatures, ranging from 10°C to 25°C (50°F to 77°F). The weather is generally stable, with occasional rain showers. The fall foliage adds a picturesque quality to the landscape.

- Advantages: Autumn is an excellent time for cultural exploration and culinary experiences, as harvest festivals and wine tastings are in full swing.

Tourist crowds thin out, providing a more relaxed travel experience.

- Events: Notable events include the International Festival of Film in Venice, various truffle fairs in regions like Umbria and Piedmont, and the grape harvest festivals throughout wine-producing areas.

Winter (December to February)

- Weather: Winters can be cold, with temperatures ranging from 0°C to 15°C (32°F to 59°F) depending on the region. Snow is common in northern Italy and mountainous areas, while southern Italy experiences milder weather.

- Advantages: Winter is ideal for experiencing Italy's festive holiday season, with Christmas markets, New Year celebrations, and winter sports opportunities in the Alps and Dolomites. Cities are beautifully decorated, and museums and attractions are less crowded.

- Events: Major winter events include the Christmas markets in cities like Florence and Rome, Carnival celebrations, particularly in Venice, and various winter sports competitions.

What to Pack

Packing appropriately for Italy involves considering the weather, planned activities, and regional differences.

Spring

- Clothing: Light layers are recommended, including a mix of short and long-sleeve shirts, a light jacket or sweater, and comfortable trousers. A raincoat or umbrella is useful for occasional showers.

- Footwear: Comfortable walking shoes are essential for exploring cities and historic sites. Consider packing a pair of dressier shoes for dining out or attending events.

- Accessories: Sunglasses and a hat for sunny days, as well as a light scarf for cooler evenings.

Summer

- Clothing: Pack light, breathable fabrics such as cotton and linen. Include summer essentials like shorts, tank tops, and dresses. A swimsuit is necessary for beach visits or poolside lounging.

- Footwear: Comfortable sandals or walking shoes are ideal for both city exploration and beach outings. Flip-flops are useful for the beach or pool areas.

- Accessories: Sun protection items such as sunscreen, sunglasses, and a wide-brimmed hat. A reusable water bottle is helpful for staying hydrated.

Autumn

- Clothing: Layered clothing works well, including sweaters, long-sleeve shirts, and a medium-weight jacket. A warm coat might be needed, particularly in northern regions or at higher elevations.

- Footwear: Sturdy walking shoes or boots are suitable for varied weather conditions. Waterproof options can be beneficial if rain is anticipated.

- Accessories: An umbrella or raincoat, and a scarf or gloves if traveling to colder areas.

Winter

- Clothing: Pack warm clothing, including a heavy coat, sweaters, thermal layers, and long pants. In northern Italy and mountainous areas, consider packing thermal wear and waterproof gear.

- Footwear: Insulated and waterproof boots are recommended for cold or snowy conditions. Comfortable shoes for indoor use are also necessary.

- Accessories: Warm hats, gloves, and scarves. Don't forget items like a travel-sized umbrella and moisturizers to combat the dry winter air.

Weather Conditions

Italy's weather varies significantly from region to region, influenced by its diverse geography.

Northern Italy

- Climate: Generally experiences a temperate climate with cold winters and warm to hot summers. The Alps and northern Apennines can receive heavy snowfall in winter, ideal for skiing and winter sports.

- Typical Conditions: Winter temperatures can drop below freezing, while summer temperatures in cities like Milan and Venice can reach the high 20s to low 30s°C (70s to 80s°F). Rainfall is relatively frequent, especially in the spring and autumn.

Central Italy

- Climate: Characterized by a Mediterranean climate with hot, dry summers and mild, wet winters. The Tuscan countryside and cities like Florence experience more moderate temperatures compared to northern regions.

- Typical Conditions: Summer temperatures are warm, ranging from 25°C to 35°C (77°F to 95°F), while winter temperatures are cooler but rarely below freezing. Rain is more common in the autumn and winter months.

Southern Italy and the Islands

- Climate: Known for its Mediterranean climate with hot, dry summers and mild, wet winters. The coastal regions and islands, such as Sicily and Sardinia, benefit from a warmer climate year-round.

- Typical Conditions: Summers are hot, often exceeding 30°C (86°F), while winters are mild with temperatures rarely dropping below 10°C (50°F). Rainfall is less frequent compared to northern Italy but can occur, particularly in the winter months.

Coastal Regions

- Climate: Coastal areas experience milder temperatures due to the moderating effect of the sea. Coastal summer temperatures are typically more pleasant, and winters are mild.

- Typical Conditions: Summer temperatures range from 25°C to 30°C (77°F to 86°F), and winter temperatures usually stay above freezing. Coastal areas also experience a more consistent humidity level throughout the year.

By understanding the best times to visit, packing appropriately for the season, and being aware of regional weather conditions, you can plan your trip to Italy effectively. This preparation ensures you're equipped to handle various weather scenarios and enjoy your travel experience to the fullest.

CHAPTER 13. CONCLUSION

Italy is a land of extraordinary beauty, history, and culture. As you embark on your journey through this enchanting country, you will encounter a tapestry of experiences that reflect its rich heritage and vibrant present. This guide has been designed to help you navigate the diverse facets of Italian travel, from the best times to visit and essential packing tips to local customs and practical advice.

Italy's regions each offer their own unique allure, from the historic grandeur of Rome and the artistic treasures of Florence to the serene landscapes of Tuscany and the dramatic coastlines of the Amalfi Coast. Embrace the diversity of the country, and allow yourself to be captivated by the charm of each destination.

Understanding the seasonal variations will greatly enhance your travel experience. Spring and autumn provide mild weather and fewer crowds, ideal for exploring Italy's rich cultural and historical sites. Summer brings lively festivals and beach opportunities, though it also means higher temperatures and more tourists. Winter, with its festive spirit and colder climate, offers a different but equally rewarding experience, especially in terms of holiday celebrations and winter sports.

Respecting local customs and etiquette is crucial for a positive travel experience. Italy's cultural practices, from polite greetings to appropriate dining manners, reflect its deep-rooted traditions. By following these social norms, you'll not only show respect but also connect more meaningfully with the locals.

Italy's culinary landscape is a significant highlight of any visit. From world-renowned pasta and pizza to regional specialties and local wines, the country's food culture is a celebration of tradition and flavor. Exploring food markets, participating in local festivals, and savoring authentic dishes will enhance your travel experience and deepen your appreciation for Italian cuisine.

Navigating Italy's transportation system, understanding currency and banking, and staying informed about health and safety will contribute to a smoother and more enjoyable trip. Practical knowledge of these aspects ensures that you can focus on the pleasures of your journey without unnecessary stress.

Ultimately, Italy's allure lies not just in its famous landmarks but in the moments of serendipity and personal discovery you encounter. Savor the unique experiences, engage with the culture, and allow yourself to be inspired by the beauty and warmth of Italy. Your journey through this remarkable country will undoubtedly be filled with unforgettable memories and enriching encounters. Buon viaggio!

Printed in Great Britain
by Amazon